FALCONRY

WITH CHAPTERS ON:

THE PEREGRINE, PASSAGE HAWKS, ADVANTAGES OF, HOW CAUGHT, MODE OF TRAINING, HERON HAWKING, ROOK HAWKING, GULL HAWKING, PASSAGE HAWKS FOR GAME AND LOST HAWKS

BY

GERALD LASCELLES

British Library Cataloguing-in-Publication Data
A catalogue record for this book is available from the
British Library

CONTENTS

Falconry

'Falconry' refers to the hunting of wild quarry in its natural state and habitat by means of a trained bird of prey. There are two traditional terms used to describe a person involved in falconry: a 'falconer' flies a falcon, and an 'austringer' (a term of German origin) flies a hawk or an eagle. Falconry has a long and distinguished history, and it has been suggested that it began in Mesopotamia, with the earliest accounts dating to approximately 2000 BC. It was probably introduced to Europe around 400 AD however, when the Huns and the Alans invaded from the East. Frederick II of Hohenstaufen (a member of the Swabian dynasty in the High Middle Ages who possessed huge amounts of territory across Europe) is generally acknowledged as the most significant wellspring of traditional falconry knowledge. He is believed to have obtained firsthand knowledge of Arabic falconry during wars in the region in 1228 and 1229, in which he participated in his role as Holy Roman Emperor. Frederick is best known for his falconry treatise, *De Arte Venandi Cum Avibus* (The Art of Hunting with Birds); the first comprehensive book on falconry, as well as a substantial contribution to ornithology and zoology. Historically, falconry has always been a popular sport of the upper classes and nobility, largely due to the prerequisites of time, money and space. However, within some societies, such as the Bedouin, falconry was not practiced for recreation, but for purely practical reasons of supplementing a very limited diet. In the UK, falconry reached its zenith in the seventeenth century, but faded reasonably rapidly due to the introduction of firearms for hunting in the eighteenth and nineteenth centuries. It did witness a revival in the late nineteenth and earlier twentieth centuries however, when several falconry books were published. Interestingly, in early English falconry literature, the word 'falcon' referred to a female falcon only, while the word 'hawk' referred to a female hawk. A male hawk or falcon was referred to as a 'tercel', as it was roughly one third less than the female in size. Whilst falconry is now practiced in many countries world wide, it is less common in areas such as Australasia. In Australia, although falconry is not specifically illegal, it is illegal to keep any type of bird of prey in captivity without the appropriate permits, and in New Zealand, falconry was legalised for one species only, the Swap/Australasian harrier, in 2011. There are currently only four practicing falconers in New Zealand. However, in countries such as the UK and US today, falconry is experiencing a boom. Its popularity, through lure flying displays at country houses and game fairs, has probably never been higher in the past 300 years. It has also been the subject of a popular book *Falcon Fever,* written by Tim Gallagher in 2008. Falconry is also used for practical purposes in the modern day, the birds are taught to control other pest birds and animals in urban areas, landfills, commercial buildings, and even airports.

FALCONRY

THE PEREGRINE—PASSAGE HAWKS—
ADVANTAGES OF—HOW CAUGHT—MODE
OF TRAINING—HERON HAWKING—ROOK
HAWKING—GULL HAWKING—PASSAGE HAWKS
FOR GAME —LOST HAWKS

What the professional is to the amateur, or rather, perhaps, what the thoroughbred horse is to all other varieties of the equine race, the passage hawk is, according to species, to every other hawk which is trained, inasmuch as she is swifter, more active, more hardy, and more powerful than the nestling. That this should be so is no matter for surprise when it is recollected that the passage, or wild-caught, hawk has spent days and weeks on the wing in every kind of weather, and has killed dozens, or perhaps hundreds, of wild birds in fair flight, while the nestling has only gained what power of wing she possesses from some three or four weeks of flying at hack, and since that time has been flown at from two to three birds a day, and that only when the weather was fine. Moreover, though we cannot definitely account for this, the temper of the wild-caught hawk is, as a rule, far gentler and more amiable, when once she is tamed, than is that of a hawk taken from the nest; and, while the latter are rarely free from the horrible trick of screaming, that vice is almost unknown among passage hawks.

These differences in temper were well understood by Symon Latham, who published in 1615 his book called 'The Faulcon's Lure and Cure' (which is to this day the best English work on falconry ever written), and who says in conclusion of a chapter on eyess falcons : ' But leaving to speak any more of these kinde of scratching hawks, that I did never love should come too neere my fingers, and to returne unto the curteous and faire conditioned haggard faulcon whose gallant disposition I know not how to extoll or praise so sufficiently as she deserves.'

What the falconers of ancient days thus recorded is abundantly confirmed by the practice of their successors in modern times. The passage hawk, as every wild-caught peregrine is termed, with the distinction of ' haggard' when she is captured in the mature plumage—perhaps aged several years—has proved herself, in our own experience, the superior to the eyess in every kind of flight to which the peregrine can be put. But, moreover, there are many flights such as those at the heron and the rook, for which the passage hawk alone is well adapted, and of which the eyess, as a rule, is not capable. It is true that there have been many eyesses which have been fairly good rook hawks—in one or two instances they have even taken the heron ' on the passage,' but such hawks were exceptional ones.

To obtain a team of, say, six good hawks that would take the heron, or even the rook, in the rough winds of March as he passes to and from his feeding-grounds, it would be necessary to train and test at least twenty eyesses ; but a better result would be obtained from the training, in experienced hands, of ten well-caught passage falcons. And, again, even if the trainer of the eyesses were to succeed in producing hawks that took rooks or herons fairly well, he could never hope that they would emulate the style and dash with which their wild-bred congeners accomplished the feat; nor, above all, would he be as independent of weather as are those who use the hardy passage hawk, which seems to glory in a gale and laugh at the bitterness of the north-east wind.

For game hawking the passage hawk requires both time and careful training, and here, perhaps because of the difficulty of managing the wild-caught hawk, the eyess holds her own. Yet even when the best possible eyesses are being flown—hawks that may be trusted to kill three and four head of game every day—if there be in the stud a passage falcon that will wait on high and steadily, she will so eclipse the eyess for style and pace, and above all in ' footing qualities,' i.e. accuracy of striking her quarry, that there is no comparison between the pleasure which is afforded by the flights shown by the two hawks. Probably no game hawk has beaten the record of ' Parachute,' as shown on page 251, of 146 head of game in five months, or of 'Vesta,' also the property of the Old

Hawking Club, who has killed 297 grouse (besides other game in numbers) during her nine years. Yet in nearly every season that such hawks have flown they have had to take the second place, as regards brilliancy of execution and deadliness of stoop and style, to some one or two of the passage hawks which have accompanied them to their hawking ground, and this will ever be the case when both varieties are given a fair trial.

Tiercel on partridge

Naturally, the hawk which has spent so long a period in a wild state, during which she has imbibed a holy horror of man and all his works, regarding him as her natural foe, is very much more difficult to train at first than the nestling, which requires at any rate little or no taming, and whose idea of man is that he is a being created in order to bring food to hawks. First, however, how are passage hawks to be obtained ? They may be caught doubtless in many parts of the United Kingdom, where, every autumn about the middle of October, peregrines appear, for a day or two, on ground where they certainly do not breed, and where they are very seldom seen at other times. Thus falcons have been taken, at huts specially put out for the purpose, both in Northamptonshire and on the downs of Wiltshire. These no doubt were stragglers from the great army of birds of all kinds and descriptions which annually migrates from north to south at the commencement of winter. Upon the outskirts of this army hang the falcons and other raptorial birds ; whether they are themselves following the same migratory instinct that urges onward the other innumerable varieties of birds, or whether they are simply following their food as it changes its quarters, it is impossible to say.

In North Brabant in Holland, near to Eindhoven, there is a vast wild plain or heath, and this plain appears to lie in the very centre of the track which the great concourse of migratory birds follows. Wild fowl of every kind, cranes, larks, linnets, all varieties of birds may be seen, during October and November, passing over this plain and steadily pursuing their route southwards. Here, too, come the falcons, first the haggards and tiercels, after them the young falcons of the year, and here from time immemorial have they been captured for hawking purposes. On the edge of the heath lies the little town of Valkenswaard, which takes its very name from the falcons, that in old days were its staple article of trade. Therein reside certain families of men who from generation to generation, as far back as history goes, have been falconers and catchers of falcons. Some hundred years ago, even, there were from twenty to thirty huts put out at Valkenswaard for the capture of hawks during the autumn passage, and the little town could boast of the like number of men skilled in training hawks. In those days a sort of fair was held after the migration was over, which was attended by the chief falconers of various noblemen and princes from every country in Europe. The hawks that had been caught were sold by auction, and rare prices were occasionally paid for very choice specimens, with such a competition as took place under the circumstances described. Ichabod ! The glory has departed. Some three huts now supply all the wants of the hawking world. They are under the management of one family, the Mollens, the head of which, Adrian Mollen, was formerly head falconer to the King of Holland, and his customers average annually some half-a-dozen only, mostly Englishmen, with a Frenchman or two added to them. The actual instrument which is used in taking the hawks is the bow-net, which has been fully described in the chapter on hacking and training eyesses at page 241. Two or perhaps three of these nets are set out at about a hundred yards each from the falconer's hut, into which lead the strong lines by which they are worked.

The hut itself is a very simple affair, partly sunk in the ground and partly built of turfs and sods covered with heather. The roof is very often made of an old cartwheel, which is well covered over with heath arid turf, so that the hut itself looks exactly like a small natural mound on the surface of the plain, and perfectly conceals the falconer even from the sharp eyes of a bird of prey.

The bait for each of the bow-nets is a live pigeon, which is kept in a cleverly constructed little house built of turves, with a hanging curtain over the door, made of a heather sod, so that when the long line, which is attached to the pigeon by soft buckskin jesses, is pulled by the falconer the curtain gives way and allows the bird to be drawn out. This line passes through an eye in the head of an iron pin, which is driven into the ground exactly in the centre of the bow-net, so that the falconer knows, whether he can see it or not, that when the pigeon's line is pulled taut and checks, the bird itself is on the ground exactly in the middle of the net.

A fourth pigeon inhabits a similar little house immediately in front of the hut, and about fifty yards from it. The line from this pigeon passes over the top of a light pole about twenty feet high, so that when this line is pulled the pigeon is raised to that height and flies well out so as to be easily seen. This pigeon is intended to serve as a lure and attract a hawk from a distance.

Sometimes it happens that the falconer will catch, early in the season, an old or a bad plumaged falcon that he does not think highly of for hawking purposes. Such a falcon he will set out, hooded, with a line attached to her, passing over a pole just as in the case of the lure pigeon. A few feet in front of the hawk is fastened to the line a bunch of feathers, so that when the line is pulled tight the hawk is lifted to the top of the pole and flies round with the bunch of feathers in front of her, looking from a distance exactly like a hawk in full pursuit of, and on the point of catching, some quarry. This forms a most attractive lure to a wild hawk, which is almost certain to pause in her flight and lower her pitch to join in the fray.

Last of all comes the most important adjunct to the apparatus, in the shape of a butcher bird, or grey shrike, which is used as a watch-dog or sentinel to give notice of the approach of a hawk. These curious little birds are always on the alert and on the look-out for birds of prey ; their power of vision is most marvellous, far beyond the reach of any human eye. They can detect a falcon, which minutes afterwards will come into sight as a tiny black speck, high in the heavens. Two of these shrikes are generally used, tethered upon mounds near the hut, with a little house, like those in which the pigeons are kept, to shelter them. As soon as they see a hawk they will chatter and scream, pointing steadily in the direction of the bird's approach. An experienced falconer can tell fairly well from the action of his butcher bird what species of hawk is in view. More alarm will be shown at the approach of a goshawk than of any other variety, while at tiercels or merlins his gestures are those of absurd indignation and defiance.

Everything being then prepared, the falconer will arrive at his hut and have all in readiness by daybreak. Early morning is the best time for catching hawks, and the passage for the day is over by three o'clock as a rule. With a good stock of tobacco and some occupation such as net-making or cobbling, to while away the many weary hours of waiting, he establishes himself inside his hut; presently, if all goes well, his butcher birds will chatter, point, and warn him to be on the look-out. Far away, it may be, he sees a tiny speck, which he believes to be a peregrine. At any rate he pulls the line attached to the pole hawk, and soon brings up the wild bird to rather closer quarters. Should it be a peregrine such as he desires to capture, he drops the line attached to the pole hawk, which at once subsides to the ground, and draws that which lifts the pigeon to the top of the pole, and lets it fly well out. At this pigeon the wild hawk most likely ' comes with a rattle,' but at the nick of time the falconer drops the line, and the frightened bird will bolt into its little hut for safety. Angry and disappointed, the wild hawk will shoot into the air and give a circle round to see what has become of her prey. At this juncture the falconer pulls out the pigeon attached to one or other end (according to the direction of wind and position of the hawk) of his bow-net. The wild falcon's blood is up ; she has been disappointed once, and she dashes like lightning on to the pigeon, which she imagines to be the one that just escaped her. Of course she has no difficulty in taking it, and as she is killing it the falconer steadily draws the line till it checks at the head of the iron pin in the centre of the net. One pull of the net line and the hawk is safely caught. As rapidly as possible she is taken out of the net, a rufter hood is placed on her head—that is to say, a light, comfortable hood, open at the back, and easy for a hawk to feed through—she is then placed in a ' sock,' which is simply the leg of an old stocking, which pins her wings to her sides and acts as a strait-waistcoat, making it impossible for her to move or to struggle. Jesses are placed on her legs, the points are taken off her beak and claws, and she is left to lie quiet until the time arrives for leaving the hut and going home.

Two hawks in one day is unusually good fortune. More often the falconer sits day after day without any luck at all. Sometimes it happens that from something going wrong with his tackle, or from some such cause, he misses the hawk. This is a serious reverse, for he will not easily get the chance to catch the same bird again. Such a mishap occurred to Mollen, senior, in 1872. He had just caught a falcon, and was taking her out of the net when there came up, attracted by the pigeon, an exceedingly fine dark falcon. It was too late to hide ; but when, an hour or so afterwards, she again appeared on the scene, and he pulled out the lure pigeon, all that resulted was, that after a shy stoop the falcon followed the line at the height of a yard or two right from the net to the hut, spread her wings, and sailed away. There were many wild fowl on the heath at the time, and he could see this grand hawk day after day chasing and killing them in the finest style, till his mouth fairly watered to catch her. In vain did he try all his arts ; every time he showed his lure the crafty bird would sail along the extended string; as if to show how well she understood the game, and then would bid him good-bye. Worst of all, she would brook no intruder on her hunting grounds, and day after day as other falcons passed and began to stoop to the pigeon, she would descend upon them from the clouds, and after a buffeting match would drive them away. Mollen was in despair, the season was slipping away, and his business being lost At last he took his gun to the hut, having made up his mind to shoot the hawk as a last resource and free himself from the incubus. Hour after hour he sat with gun in readiness—a strange position, indeed, for a falconer. But that day she came not, nor the next, and at last the gun was laid aside and the hawk catching went on as before.

Passage hawk under bow-net

At the end of the week one of Mollen's sons who was working a hut many miles away returned home with his catch. He had not much to boast of, except one, ' a real beauty.' Hardly had the old man set eyes on her than he recognised his tormentor—unmistakable from her size, dark plumage, and beauty. She had gone straight to the other hut after plaguing him the last day he saw her, but never having been frightened at that place was less suspicious and so was caught. This hawk came into the possession of the Old Hawking Club, where she was known as ' the Duck-killer,' and was one of the grandest hawks for temper, flying qualities, and steadiness that the Club have ever owned, killing over forty rooks her first season. She was eventually lost when flying rooks at Feltwell in Norfolk, and it is to be hoped became the mother of falcons as good as herself on some wild cliff in North Britain, or Scandinavia.

But to return to the freshly caught falcon. Her captor will have little difficulty in carrying her home on his fist ; so dazed and terrified will she be by her novel situation that she will sit like a hawk of stone. On arrival the hawk may be temporarily set on the perch with any others that have been lately caught, or, better still, fastened securely to a soft grass mound (which sometimes takes the place of the sock); but the sooner she is taken in hand, the better. The directions which have been already given for the training of the freshly taken-up eyess will apply in this case also, but it must never be forgotten that the passage hawk has hitherto spent her days in avoiding men as her natural enemies, and that it will take much time, care, and gentleness ere this terror and aversion can be overcome. A single impatient action or hasty gesture may undo the work of days, and the man who tries to tame a wild-caught hawk should possess a temper which is under perfect command and a patience which is ' above proof.'

The first step is to take the hawk on hand and to handle her gently, stroking her with a feather or some such thing, to accustom her to being taken hold of and handled. Hawks differ marvellously at this stage of their education. Some will display the most passionate temper, will fight, bite, even scream, and dash themselves about like passionate children. Such as these are usually the easiest to deal with ; their passion soon abates and generally develops into a fine, generous temper. Some sit like statues—immovable, indifferent, resenting no handling, noticing no food—such are difficult hawks to train, and only time and patience, added to experience, will train these, though it can be, and annually is, done. Gradually the hawk will become reconciled to the touch, to the sound of the human voice, and will in a few days comport herself more like a tame bird and less like a wild beast. Most of this work is done at night; and the best method of training wild-caught, or indeed any other birds, is to deal with them at night and to tame, them by depriving them of their natural rest and by handling them by lamplight, which dazes them and takes away half their power of resistance. Where time is an object, hawks are kept awake for the whole night for three or four nights together, and by such treatment a hawk may be tamed in about four days. Such haste is rarely needed, and in ordinary cases any hawk may be got into good order in reasonable time by taking her on hand, say, from seven in the evening until eleven at night j and, indeed, a man may have two .or three hawks on the perch by his side, and by taking them in hand alternately bring them all on together at the same rate.

It is very important, if the most is to be made of passage hawks, that each one should be taken in hand as soon as she is caught, and tamed at once. This is not always easily managed, and sometimes several birds are left to stand idle for many days while others are being caught. This leads to many faults, always causes delay (sometimes very great delay) in the training and entering of such hawks, and not unfrequently ruins them altogether.

The great secret in successful training of passage hawks is *to get food into them* by fair means. This is by no means so easy as it appears to be, and requires no little skill in the way of handling the hawk so as to get her to bite at the food which is held on to her feet, and to continue feeding after she has once begun. The room must be perfectly quiet, there must be no changes of light or distant sounds heard, or the hawk's attention will at once be arrested and she will leave off feeding. There is also great knack in getting her to pull at the meat without being frightened. Adrian Mollen boasts, not without reason, that he can get a quarter of a crop more into any hawk after any other man has done his best with her. It is very important that hawks shall be well fed ; they will lose their wild condition quite fast enough from the change of food, the numerous shocks to their nervous system, and the loss of exercise ; but if they are allowed to get down too low they will never recover their power or their courage. If all goes well, however, in a few days the hawk will feed well and boldly through the rufter hood, will allow herself to be handled, and will feel more at home on the fist. The rufter hood should now be removed by candle-light, and the hawk induced to feed bare-headed. A hood of ordinary make can also be placed on her, and she can be frequently hooded and unhooded and broken carefully to the hood in the same way as eyesses are treated. When she sits quiet and bare-headed by candle-light, the same lesson may be repeated by daylight, and ere its close the hawk will jump to the hand for her food—at first a short distance only, afterwards the full length of the leash—and will do so promptly and briskly as soon as the meat is shown her. All this takes a good deal of time and patience, but anything like hurry is to be avoided, or the hawk will probably go back rapidly as soon as she is taken out into the open air. So long as a little progress, be it ever so little, is made every day, the falconer should be content, and not endeavour to hurry his more backward, shy tempered birds in order to keep pace with one or two good-tempered ones that ' never look behind them,' and almost train themselves.

As soon as the hawk will feed fearlessly on the hand bareheaded she should be entered to the lure: this at the first outset must, in the case of wild-caught hawks, consist of a live pigeon. The moment the hawk seizes it the falconer should twist its neck, so as to kill it instantaneously and painlessly, and the hawk should be allowed to break into and eat it while still warm.

Many passage falcons are very stupid and troublesome to enter to the lure just at first. The process of taming and training them seems to have completely transformed their nature and driven all recollection of their past life out of their minds. It is very curious to notice how the young eyess, which has no fear at all of man or nervousness at its surroundings, will, almost to a certainty, seize and kill instinctively the first live pigeon shown to it, though it has never killed a bird before ; while the passage hawk, which has, perhaps, chased and killed hundreds of wild birds during its life, and has subsisted on nothing else, will sometimes sit and blink stupidly at a pigeon within a few feet of it, as though it had never seen such a creature before. A little patience will overcome this difficulty also, and as soon as the hawk will seize and kill a pigeon within doors, and feed quietly upon it without fear of the falconer, she may be tried out of doors on a long string with the pigeon similarly confined. Should she behave equally well this time also she may be trusted to fly loose. A good deal of care must be exercised the first few times she is flown, for if any little thing should go wrong and upset the hawk's equanimity it may become a difficult matter to take her up at once ; and if she is at large, even for an hour or two, out of control, her wild ways will at this stage return to her with great rapidity. She should be very sharp-set, and for the first trial it will be quite enough to call her from the fist of an assistant (who must not be a perfect stranger to her) about a hundred yards to the falconer. One or two stoops will be enough, and she should then be allowed to feed on the lure. As soon as the hawk behaves well and flies keenly, the use of live pigeons should be abandoned, and the hawk trained to the dead lure. In former days it was supposed that passage hawks could not be trained to dead lures until they had been in work for a long time, but we have proved this to be a fallacy, and that it is, with care and good management, quite as possible to get passage hawks to come to the dead lure as it is to train eyesses to it. The early education cannot in either case be carried on without the sacrifice of two or three pigeons. These should be killed instantaneously the moment the hawk touches them, and all unnecessary cruelty avoided. But as soon as these first stages of the falcon's education are completed the ' live lure' should become a thing unknown, except in cases of emergency, such as a lost hawk.

As soon as the passage falcon flies well and steadily to the lure, stooping at it for seven or eight minutes at a time, she should be entered to the quarry at which she is to be flown. It is a very bad plan to keep hawks that are fit to be entered flying on at the lure day after day, for weeks together. Such hawks will become very tame and very handy, but they will lose all that dash which is the special charm of the passage hawk, and will become so wedded to the lure that they will fly at nothing else.[1]

The quarry which, as a rule, the passage hawk alone is capable of taking, is the heron ' on the passage'; to enter her to this quarry she should first be allowed to take and kill a few large-sized fowls. If she should seize and tackle these powerful birds with determination, she will have no hesitation in binding to a heron if ever she shall get to close quarters enough to do so. After this education she must be flown at a bagged heron, first in a string and afterwards loose and at some distance from her. During these lessons her beak and talons must be cut very short and well rounded off, so that beyond seizing the heron she can do him no injury before the falconer runs to save him. Having once ' bound to him' the falcon must be fed upon some food which she relishes, and after a lesson or two of this kind she should be fit to fly at a wild heron.

Heron hawking, however—sad as it is to record it—must be written down as a sport almost extinct in England. To catch a heron with a hawk as it rises from the stream where it may be feeding is easy enough ; any nestling that has been well entered, even the short-winged goshawk, can do this to an absolute certainty every time that it is brought near enough to the quarry; but this is not heron hawking. To arrive at this sport the following conditions are necessary. A heronry of large size, situated far from any river or feeding-ground, so that the herons pass continually to and from the nearest river to the heronry, and pass also over some vast open space of ground suitable to be ridden over and wide enough to afford a flight of at least two miles ere the heron could reach either a sheltering wood or a piece of water into which he will dive like a duck. Nay, we have known a heron to put in even to a sheepfold when hard pressed on an open field !

[1] But it is necessary to observe that the passage hawk must at first only be entered to quarry which she cannot easily carry (unless, indeed, extraordinary pains are taken to tame her). Otherwise she is very likely to lift any light bird (such as a pigeon), and, though not actually wild at first, she becomes so frightened at being followed with a bird in her foot, which she repeatedly carries, that she becomes unapproachable.

Such conditions as these were well fulfilled at Didlington in Norfolk, which was for many years the scene of the sport of the High Ash Club. But here, even so long ago as 1838, the draining of the fenland and breaking up and cultivation of the open heaths so limited the area in which it was possible to pursue the sport that blank days became more and more common, and eventually the club was broken up. Better still were the conditions under which the sport was pursued at the Loo in Holland, where the heronry was of vast size, and the country surrounding it even better than at Didlington. Here heron hawking was pursued on a princely scale, the joint establishments of the King of Holland and of the English Club being equal to any emergency, and some idea can be obtained of the sport which they obtained when it is recorded that in one year (1852) the hawks took no fewer than 292 herons, while for eight years in succession they actually averaged 178 herons annually.[1]

---

[1] See Schlegel's Traité de Fauconnerie, 1844.

Of course so large a number of herons taken in the breeding season would very soon ruin the finest heronry in the world, but it was the practice to save and liberate every heron that was taken, and it was a point of honour with the members of the Club to ride hard enough to be handy at the finish, so as to make sure that the heron should not be injured. When liberated a small copper ring was fixed to his leg with the date of his capture written on it, and herons have been taken with as many as three and four of these rings on their legs.[1]

The method of conducting the sport is as follows. The falconers with their hawks are placed at intervals of half a mile, in two or three parties, down wind of the heronry, and at some considerable distance from it. As the heron passes homewards with his crop full of fish, he must pass within sufficiently close distance of one or the other of these parties. As soon as he is well past, and up wind of the hawks, they are hooded off. Probably the heron is two hundred yards away, and at least a hundred yards high, and with such a start as this he can set to work to ring into the air with confidence. It is useless for him to attempt to reach the heronry, which is dead up wind, while he has such pursuers as these behind him. Below him is no protecting covert, and therefore his only resources are the clouds above him. Ring after ring he makes, mounting into the air in long spiral curves. Ring after ring do the hawks make after him, tearing into the wind for perhaps half a mile without a turn, and then swinging round in a great circle that sends them higher and higher. At last one hawk is over him, though at such a height we cannot distinguish the distances between them ; but we can see her shut her wings and drive like a bullet at the heron. A rapid shift, and the hawk has fallen many hundreds of feet below her quarry, but, shooting up with the same impetus, at once sets to work to ring into the wind, so as to regain her lost advantage. During this time the second falcon has climbed almost out of sight above her mate and her quarry, and can be just distinguished poising herself for a terrific stoop. The good heron can just, but only just, avoid it, and that with the loss of a few feathers and a downward sweep that sacrifices some minutes of the hard ringing by which the height he is now at was attained. This sweep gives a chance to the first hawk and down she comes, pressing the heron hard—so hard that as her mate follows her at an interval of a second or two he is hit heavily. In another moment one hawk has bound to him, and ere the struggle can commence the other has joined in the fray, and all three birds steadily descend to the ground. The wind has carried them for at least a mile from where they were hooded off, and that, too, at a pace as good as a horseman cares to gallop over fairly rough ground with his eyes in the air.

---

[1] See Falconry in the British Isles, p. 81.

'A CLOSE SHAVE'

Old hawks will always let go the heron as they approach the ground, so as to avoid the concussion, and will renew the attack the instant that they are safely landed. Some falcons are a little slow in ' making in' to a heron on the ground, and in this way have been badly stabbed. If the heron has time afforded to him to collect himself and get into a fighting attitude he is a dangerous opponent, but the fables of hawks spitting themselves as they stoop upon beaks upturned in the air are myths which have no foundation in fact. A heron on the ground is, however, a formidable enemy, and when hawks are flown at a bagman it is essential that his beak be muzzled by being cased in a double piece of soft elder, one for each mandible, or mischief is sure to ensue.

It is absolutely necessary that hawks should be well entered to herons and should be kept to this flight alone. So far as we know, there is hardly any place left in England where a heronry exists with suitable country round it so that one or even two flights could be obtained daily. It is not, therefore, worth the while of any falconer to set aside a cast or two of his best hawks for a flight which, noble as it is, he could not obtain with any certainty. Probably at the Loo—although even there much of the country is enclosed and cultivated—very good sport could be obtained, but it is thirty-six years since the cry of ' A la vol' echoed in the domain of ' Het Loo,' and it is doubtful if there are more than two or three falconers now alive who have seen the heron taken 'a la haute volee.' Heron hawking must, for the present, be looked upon as a thing of the past ; but hawks are still trained annually that are as capable of this noble flight as any that ever have been reclaimed by man, and it needs only a little enterprise to reinstate this, the most magnificent form of falconry, if it could meet with the same cordial support, and be organised under those Royal auspices that were extended to it forty years ago.

Perhaps even superior to heron hawking was the flight at the kite, for which passage falcons combined with gerfalcons were used. It is many years since kites were common enough in England to be an object of sport, and the method of flying them is more particularly described in a subsequent chapter on the gyrfalcon.

The modern substitute for heron hawking is the flight at the rook, and it is by no means a bad one. Rook hawking is the finest form of the sport that is nowadays readily available, provided that it is carried out in a proper manner, in a good country, and with the best of hawks. Rooks, just like herons, may be caught in a bad country by very inferior hawks. In the autumn, in a country where the fields are large, the fences mall, and the hedgerow timber scarce, rooks may be driven into covert and (possibly) caught, after a chase partaking of the nature of a rat hunt, by almost any hawk that has courage enough to go straight and hard at her quarry. But this is not rook hawking. The falcons that have beaten down rook after rook into fences or covert in enclosed country in November would find themselves at a sad nonplus if they were hooded off at an old cock rook travelling away over the wide downs of Wilts or Berks in the teeth of a March north-easter. The proper time for this sport is the month of March or early April when the hen birds are in the rookery and the cocks are travelling great distances in search of food. A very open country is requisite. The chalk downs of the south of England are, generally speaking, the best. Parts of Salisbury Plain, the downs near Lambourne and Ashdown, and near Brighton, at Royston, and other parts of Cambridgeshire are capital country, and in fact, wherever a clear open space of a mile can be found rooks may be flown with success. The difficulty is to find any country where flights can be obtained day after day; for this quarry becomes very crafty, and the appearance of the well-known hawking party over the sky-line is enough to send every rook in the plain below scurrying to his home if the visits have been too frequent to the same portion of country.

A flight may be obtained wherever the quarry is found far enough from covert, whether following the plough, feeding on new-sown corn, or on open downs. After rain with a south-west wind they will be found on the turf downs, but in dry, cold weather they will haunt sheepfolds or villages, and flights are not so easily obtained. The best flights are obtained at rooks ' upon the passage'—that is to say, passing regularly from the rookery to some favourite feeding ground across an open stretch of ground. Such a slip is generally a pretty long one ; the rook at any rate is well on the wing, and a fine flight is almost a certainty. It is most essential that the hawks should be slipped dead up wind at the rook. This is a cardinal rule, and must never be transgressed, although with a very good hawk liberties may be taken now and then. If the slip is down wind, or so nearly on a side wind that by a swerve right or left the rook can get to leeward of the hawk, he will dash away down wind at a pace that will leave all riders far behind. Although the hawk will follow him just as fast, it will be a stern chase and a long one, and in no country that we are aware of is there room for a flight of this kind to end successfully ; the result *must* be a long uninteresting chase without a stoop, with the rook safely ensconced in covert at the end, some miles from the falconer. The hawk is there with no one to take her down to the lure, and is left to dash after any fresh quarry as soon as she gets her wind, and thus is lost.

If the slip be dead in wind, the rook cannot go straight away from the falcon, who is better at flying into the wind than he is ; but he will at first do his best to escape her by flying up wind, rising all the time to keep above her; thus ere she can reach him both birds will have attained a considerable height. But as soon as the hawk gains her pitch fairly over the rook, he can no longer carry on in the teeth of the gale, but must turn down wind, thus passing under the falcon and giving her the chance of her stoop, and also passing by all the horsemen, who, up to this point, have been following the flight up wind. Although the rest of the flight will be down the wind, the hawk will have so far got the advantage that she will put in stoop after stoop, and thus the horsemen will be able to keep up fairly well, and, at any rate, to see a pretty flight with many stoops, far different from a long down-wind stern chase, and should, moreover, be near enough at the finish (if their horses can gallop, and they can ride them) to secure the hawk, if, perchance, she is, after all, beaten to some covert, Let it then be considered an inviolable rule in rook hawking and all similar flights that the hawk be flown dead in the wind at the quarry, just as in game hawking the birds should be flushed dead down wind under the hawk.

It is not always an easy matter to enter falcons at rooks. The quarry is distasteful to them because it is difficult to catch, difficult to master when on the ground, and disagreeable to eat. Many hawks can only be brought to fly them by very skilful management, and at first all must be extra sharp set when first entered to them. No hawk, however, can be made to show any sport by the process of starvation, and, though she may be so reduced by hunger as to dash keenly at anything alive, yet her strength will fail her directly she is asked to climb into the wind over a rapidly mounting rook. The famous hawk ' Bois-le-Duc' was a striking instance of this unwillingness to fly rooks. Throughout her training she had shown such power, speed, and dash that it was clear she was a hawk of no mean order. When entered at bagged rooks she would dash at them and take them out of sheer devilry ; and when first flown at wild rooks she would tear away over them, in spite of wind, snow, or any disadvantages, but having them once at her mercy would disdain to stoop and finish her work. To have starved her into flying would have been to sacrifice her great powers or to lower her to the level of an ordinary falcon. Instead of this she was flown in a string at bagged rooks, and the moment she seized them a fresh-killed pigeon was thrust under the wing of the rook, and the falcon fed upon it. After a time or two she began to think that rooks were not such bad eating after all, and, being slipped at a wild one, brought it down in splendid style. The same process was repeated, and the lesson was learnt. After that day Bois-le-duc was slipped at sixty consecutive rooks, which she killed with but a single miss during that whole season, a feat which has never been rivalled by any other hawk. For some time the greatest care was paid to her condition and to her feeding, but ere long she became so wedded to her quarry that no slip was too far, no chance too bad for her, and she became, perhaps, the best rook hawk that has ever been trained.

Eyesses will sometimes take rooks very well, and there have been many good rook hawks of this kind. As a rule, they lack the dash and drive requisite for work of this kind. They will kill on fine days and in nice places, but cannot take the long slips in wild weather, and under all circumstances, that passage hawks will attempt, even if they cannot succeed, nor are they clever enough at footing to be deadly at a quarry so active in shifting as the rook. It would be almost impossible to produce a team of eyesses that would show sport to a large party, day after day, in all weathers during March and April; but with passage hawks this can annually be done.

Tiercels will fly rooks well enough, but are naturally rather more difficult to enter than falcons ; for the rook is, on the ground, almost as powerful a bird as the tiercel, and knocks him about sadly. As a rule tiercels are not entered to this quarry, but are kept for game and for magpies, &c. One of the best that ever was flown was an eyess called ' Druid,' belonging to the Hon. Cecil Duncombe, which for three years held his own and flew in his turn with a first-class team of passage falcons—no small feat indeed when the difference in size, power, and training are considered. There have been many good passage tiercels trained to rooks, of which the last was, perhaps, ' Plenipotentiary,' in 1878. Rook hawking must needs take place in very open and exposed country. It is also pursued during a very bleak stormy time of year. To insure sport it is advisable to use a light covered van in which to carry the hawks, built after the fashion of a carrier's cart, or light game waggon; the interior is fitted with perches, on which the hawks sit as well protected from weather as if they were in their mews at home. Far different is it when they are dragged over the downs on an open cadge, straining themselves to the utmost to retain their footing against the bitter breeze, and, if feeding time be delayed for an hour or two, starved by the cold till they develop many diseases of different kinds. Without warmth and protection no man can keep his hawks in the high, yet keen, condition that is essential to sport, and without the ' van,' or some such contrivance, rook hawking could not be brought to the perfection to which it has attained of late years. In their comfortable carriage the hawks are readily conveyed from place to place over a large tract of country. If rooks cannot be found in one place, the party can easily shift to another, taking the hawks with them, and in this way can cover a great deal of country.

A good horse that can gallop, but that is quiet enough to carry a hawk, is indispensable. At the end of a flight, when the falconer must needs dismount to take up his hawk, he should be tethered by a leaden weight, which is carried in a socket at the pommel of the saddle and attached to the bit by a rein. To stand well with this weight, which can be dragged if the horse bolts (i.e. do not break the bridle), and to carry a hawk well, requires a little education, and we have always found thoroughbred horses (especially young ones) more fearless and better suited to this work than any others. A good deal may be done with a very nervous horse by keeping him in a loose box with three or four live pigeons till he is thoroughly used to them, and to stand with the weight is best learned by long hacking rides with the frequent use thereof among fresh spring grass, when the horse will rapidly appreciate the luxury of being left to himself with only a slight check upon his movements, and will be only too glad to remain near the spot where his master dismounts as long as he pleases to leave him.

The following description of a flight at rooks appeared in print some years ago, but as it gives a fair idea of the sport we venture to reproduce it with slight alteration :—

Let us suppose that we are out for a day's rook hawking, and that we have arrived at our ground. All around, as far as the eye can reach, are wide rolling downs, partly cultivated, but still in a great measure clothed by the smooth virgin turf that has never known the touch of ploughshare or harrow. It is a lovely spring day ; there is a mild gentle wind from the south, with a warm sun, tempered by great fleecy clouds, throwing upon the turf huge shadows which seem to race one another from slope to slope of the downs.

We take up our position behind a stack to wait for a rook passing on his way from the rookery in the valley to the sheepfold on the hill. Presently we see one coming, toiling slowly over the shoulder of the down. Shall we fly one of the young falcons lately entered and coming on so well ? Or shall it be the old heroine of a hundred flights, victress over more than double that number of rooks, that flies now in her fourth season with all the vigour and dash she displayed in the blinding snowstorms and heavy gales of her first year ? A hundred or two of yards is far enough for a slip with a young hawk, but with a real good one a quarter of mile is not too far, while many and many a time, if the wind be right for her, the old hawk has been slipped at rooks a fair half-mile away. It looks as if this slip would be too far for a young hawk, so the handsome old falcon is taken on hand, to the delight of the whole field, not one ot whom, however large it may be, but will stay out 'just one half-hour more' when it is announced that it is the turn of old ' Bois-le-duc' to fly at the next chance that occurs.

All is hushed as the rook, a single bird, presumably a strong old cock, comes slowly up. He passes us and is going nicely on up wind when something about the party awakens his suspicions, and he gives a sudden swerve that in one second takes him about 150 yards off on a side wind. We are not to be done in this way though, and in a moment the head of our party, with the falcon on hand, dashes out at a brisk gallop down wind of the rook, which hastens on up wind. But a hundred yards or so is no matter to us with this hawk, and the moment we are fairly down wind of him the old hawk is unhooded and flung off; and the falcon is in hot pursuit of her quarry, rising with each stroke of her powerful wings till she seems to shoot upwards like an arrow from the bow. The rook has seen her, and is making his way upwards at no mean rate, but the pace of the falcon is too much for him, and ere long she is above him ; poising herself for a moment she comes, with one terrible perpendicular stoop, straight at him. It would seem as though nothing could escape ; but our rook is equal to the occasion, and with a clever shift he has dodged her attack by a good yard or more. Well done, rook ! but there is clearly now no safety for him in the air, for the falcon has shot up again with the impetus of her stoop to a height scarcely inferior to that from which she descended ; so, turning his tail to the wind, he makes all possible haste to a small patch of thorns and whins that promises a temporary shelter, having, however, on the way to evade two similar stoops from the hawk, almost as fine as the first. Alas for friend rook ! On reaching the covert he finds it already occupied by the enemy, in the shape of the excited field, who soon drive him with halloo and crack of whip from his shelter, and compel him to again seek the open. The falcon has, however, strayed a little away, so he starts with might and main to ring in spiral curves into the very clouds. After him starts the hawk, but soon finds that a really good rook, such as this is, can mount nearly as fast as she can. Up, up they go, gradually becoming smaller and smaller. Ring above ring does the falcon make, yet without getting above him, till, apparently determined to gain the victory, she starts off into the wind to make one tremendous circle that shall attain her object. Steadily into the wind she goes, the rook striving to follow her example, and appearing from below to be flying after the hawk. At length, as she almost completes the outer circumference of her circle, the rook, perhaps feeling his powers exhausted, turns down wind, and, at a great height, makes off as fast as he can go. Surely the flight is over, for the falcon is still working away, head to the wind, as hard as she can—in fact, the two birds are flying in opposite directions, half a mile apart. ' Not a bit of it!' say the initiated, who are off down wind as fast as they can ride. In another moment you see the falcon come round, and though at such a height she looks no bigger than a swallow, you can see that she is far above the rook, whilst her pace, slightly descending as she is, is almost that of a bullet. So thinks her quarry apparently, for, shutting his wings, he tries to drop like a stone into a clump of trees now nearly beneath him. Swiftly as he drops there is a swifter behind him, and down from that terrific height comes the falcon like a thunderbolt. Lord! what a stoop! By the powers, she has missed ! And now surely he must escape. But no ! shooting upwards like a rocket, the old falcon puts in one more straight swift stoop, and the rook is taken just as he enters the sanctuary which he has had his eyes on from the first. Whoo-who-op ! A grand ring! a magnificent stoop! a splendid flight!—Bravo, ' Bois-le-duc!'

Falcon flying rook

All flights are not of course so long or so good as this one, but generally afford some sport. As many as nine and ten have been killed in one day, while the total score of rooks and crows taken in the spring of 1887 by the Old Hawking Club reached 209. One year with another some 150, for the last fifteen seasons, have- generally been killed, which represents many a ringing flight, and many a brisk gallop over the breezy downs.

Another flight which taxes to the full the powers of the best passage hawks, but which is capable of affording the finest of sport, is the flight of the seagull. In many places herring and other gulls are found far inland, and in open places following the plough or feeding on the land. In 1877 the Rev. W. Willimott, a thoroughly practical falconer residing in Cornwall, trained a passage falcon, that had been entered at rooks, to this quarry with no little success. The hawk took so keenly to the gulls that she would fly them well even with flocks of rooks or other birds around her, and several very fine flights were the result. In fact, on the only occasions when the falcon was defeated the gull made good its point to the sea, but in the air the falcon had the mastery. More recently considerable success has been achieved in flying gulls upon the Yorkshire Wolds by Mr. St. Quintin. This gentleman has chiefly used tiercels for the sport, and principally passage tiercels. With these he has succeeded, on one or two occasions, in taking even the big herring gull, and, perhaps, from their greater activity, they are even better suited than falcons to the small, black-headed gull. Still, upon the whole, we think ' falcons are most likely to achieve success with seagulls. In the year 1890 Mr. St. Quintin succeeded in killing no fewer than forty-three gulls during winter and early spring, using both tiercels and falcons, and many of the flights were of the finest possible description. As gulls will put in to no sort of covert except water, this flight can be obtained in a country where any other kind of ringing flight would be impracticable. It is not an easy quarry to enter hawks to, and considerable knowledge of the condition and management of hawks is necessary. As a rule, care must be taken to avoid letting the hawks break into and eat the flesh of the gull, which is very distasteful to them, and likely to sicken them of the flight. A freshly-killed pigeon should be substituted for the gull the moment it is dead, and the hawk fed upon it, on the body of the gull where it has killed. Hawks require to be very ' fit' for this flight, as the gull's power of shifting from the stoop is marvellous, while he can also ring into the clouds very rapidly, and both hawks will need to work hard and to stoop straight and often before they can master him. Moreover the gull, especially the herring gull, bites very sharply, and the falconer must make every effort to be near enough at the close of the flight to assist his hawk, as, should a hawk be injured at first entering, it is not likely to take well to the quarry ever afterwards. It is, however, placed upon record that the seagull is perfectly within the powers of hawks of the best class, and we are of opinion that it is a flight well worthy the attention of falconers, and likely, if well managed, to afford sport of the highest kind.

The lapwing or green plover is an exceedingly difficult bird to take, so much so that it may be termed outside the category of ' quarry.' We have, however, taken a few in the spring, when they are strongest, with a very first-rate cast of passage tiercels specially trained to the flight. In August or July, when the old birds are moulting and the young have hardly arrived at their full power, they could perhaps be taken readily, but at any period of the year their powers of high-mounting and of swiftly dashing from the stoop must make them a very difficult bird to catch.

The Norfolk plover, stone curlew, or thicknee, is comparatively easy to take, but is very powerful and fights hard on the ground. It is a good quarry at which to fly hawks that are intended to fly the heron later on. It may be flown either out of the hood, or it may be marked down, and a hawk trained for game-hawking may be put up to wait on overhead and to capture it as it rises. In this way they are more easily caught. Yet occasionally a bird is met with that will shift from the first stoop, and fairly ring away into the clouds, beating, as we have sometimes seen, hawks of the very highest class that were doing their best to catch them.

The marked excellence of passage hawks at game hawking was proved for the first time in recent years in the season of 1869, when the two falconers John and Robert Barr, the one in the service of the Champagne Hawking Club and the other in that of the Marquis of Bute, met at Grandtully Castle by the invitation of the Maharajah Dhuleep Singh. The team of hawks was a very strong one, both of eyesses and of passage hawks, the latter having been caught and trained for other purposes, but soon in the skilful hands of John Barr well entered to game. The report of this clever falconer to the author of these lines was as follows :—' We are having the finest grouse hawking here that has ever been seen, killing three or four brace of grouse a day, but our hawks are *too good*—they kill every time they are flown, very often far out of sight, and are not found the same day, and often are difficult to take up after they have been left out one night.' This, no doubt, is the fault of wild-caught hawks, if they are used for any kind of hawking in which they cannot be ridden up to ; but for swiftness, style, and deadly stooping, eyesses have no chance with them. Haggards especially seem to take to waiting on very well as soon as they are thoroughly well tamed, and naturally they are most deadly at their stoop. In 1869—the year referred to above—John Barr had a very old haggard falcon named ' Granny,' that was a splendid game hawk and also very good at the heron. But the best of all his passage hawks was a falcon called 'Aurora,' so small that ' all the talent' assembled at Valkenswaard voted her to be a tiercel when first she was caught, until the veteran Adrian Mollen pointed out sundry points of distinction and proved them all to be wrong, and that she really was a tiny falcon.

Of late years ' Sibyl,' ' Bacchante' (an old haggard), and ' Elsa,' all the property of the Old Hawking Club, have proved on the Caithness moors that, however trustworthy and good eyesses may be, they cannot hold their own when tried against wild caught hawks in an open wild country with a strong swift quarry like the grouse. The fatal word ' lost,' entered against the name of many a good passage hawk in the game book, has prevented her score from reaching that of the steady-going eyess, who is rarely lost, or if lost is very easily recovered after an extra day or so at hack ; but even if the score of killed be not as great in the one case as in the other, the fine style in which the smaller number has been taken will fully balance the account between the two hawks.

In former years it was supposed that passage hawks were not fit to fly at game till after they had been for a long time in training. As long ago, however, as 1869 we saw passage tiercels waiting on perfectly in February that had been caught in the previous October and had been trained by John Barr. Since that time we have had several hawks that were perfectly steady for magpie hawking in the spring succeeding the autumn in which they were caught, and so lately as 1887 we took a magpie in April with a haggard falcon of the previous November. As a rule any passage hawk that has had a good spring season of work at rooks, &c. may be got up in condition, and after a few pigeons from the hand will wait on as well as any eyess.

Peregrines differ both in size, colour, and general appearance to an extent so great that it is sometimes almost impossible to believe that they are the same species of hawk. Some falcons of the first year are of a bright reddish cinnamon on the back, the breast being almost all of one rufous shade, blotched with dirty cream-coloured markings. Next to such a bird on the same perch will be perhaps a falcon nearly a third taller, with a rich dark brown back and wing coverts, and her breast and thighs of a bright cream colour regularly marked with very dark brown markings ; the head of such a bird will be nearly black, her thighs very evenly marked, and not a trace of red or cinnamon in her whole body. Other hawks will perhaps be there, all caught on the same passage, of every intermediate shade between these two, some nearly black, others almost the colour of a kestrel. So, too, with the adult birds. One will moult out with a beautiful pale blue back, a crop and breast almost white, with a few regular bars across the lower part. Another will have a back of the darkest blue, with head and cheeks very nearly jet black and a breast of rich salmon colour, almost rose, so strongly marked with black that, excepting that the markings run horizontally and not perpendicularly, they are almost as thick as they were in the young plumage. In old hawks pale cinnamon feathers are not uncommon about the nape of the neck, so that the hawk has somewhat the appearance of *F. Babylonicus.*

We are satisfied from close observation that it is not possible to tell from the plumage of hawks in the immature stage whether, when fully moulted out, they will be of the darker or lighter variety. As a rule those falcons which are very black in the young stage will be of a dark variety when moulted out, but we have known very light red young hawks moult to a dark variety, and *vice versâ.*

A disagreeable but a common phase of falconry is the loss of a hawk, and her recovery taxes oftentimes both the patience and the skill of the falconer. Usually the first cause of the loss is that the flight has carried both hawk and quarry far beyond the ken of their followers. In such case the falconer will follow on down wind as fast as he can to the spot where he last saw the birds, or beyond that to any point where he thinks the flight likely to have terminated. Here he will search all covert into which the quarry may have been driven and killed, from time to time showing his lure, in case the hawk may be either soaring to cool herself after a hard flight or be sitting sulky and disappointed close to where she lost her prey. If he has with him any of the field on horseback, they must be sent on straight down wind to look over all likely places, and especially to the neighbouring rookeries. If the hawk is near these or within them there will be a most unmistakable commotion, and a signal will show the falconer either that she is there or has passed that way. If the latter prove to be the case, the hawk is probably to be sought for still farther down wind of this spot. Flying another hawk to the lure will often bring up a sulky hawk, if done in an exposed place where it can be seen from all sides.

Should all these devices fail, it may be taken as certain that the hawk has killed and has gorged herself upon her quarry. In that case she will not be recovered the same day. The falconer will therefore make his arrangements to be upon the spot where the hawk was last seen or heard of before daylight the following morning. He will, with a pair of good glasses, watch the motion of every bird that moves at dawn, and these will act as his scouts^ especially in the case of rooks and crows. If he is able to reach a point where he can command a rookery from which the birds are travelling in all directions for their food, he can, sitting quietly glasses in hand, make good an immense extent of country. Should the hawk be sitting in a tree, or on her kill—nay, should she have recently killed any bird—no rook or crow will pass over it without ' mobbing,' i.e. circling round and cawing. If the rooks pass to and fro in all directions peacefully, the falconer may rely upon it that his hawk is not and has not lately been in that neighbourhood ; but if he sees one or two consecutively ' mobbing' in one place he may be sure it is worth his while to inspect it. Possibly it is only the kill of the day before, but it is an assurance that the hawk is not far off. Later in the morning he may see a lot of rooks and plovers ' sky up' in a cluster as if alarmed, and if lucky he will, near that spot, find his hawk, perhaps half gorged.

If very tame, she may even in that state come to a live pigeon, and allow him to take her up. She will almost certainly come to the pigeon, but perhaps, with a full crop and a day (or may be more) of liberty, will not allow him to take her up. He should try every plan he can think of to do so, but if he fail, then he must snare her.

If she will, as is often the case, allow him to come within twenty or thirty yards without notice, he will produce from his bag a long light line of about ioo yards (a salmon line is very good) with a peg at one end. Driving the peg into the ground, at forty yards from the hawk, as she sits plucking the pigeon, he will walk round and round, never approaching her, but thus winding the line round her legs, above the bell. As long as he keeps moving and not coming towards her the hawk will not notice him. So soon as he sees that the string is well lapped round her legs he will make quietly in towards the hawk ; but-even now, if he can, let him try to take her up, so that she may not find out she is snared. If once a hawk realises this, she is always difficult to manage, very shy of a string and of all tackle, and half spoilt. But if she attempts to leave the pigeon and fly off, the falconer must needs pull his string tight, march in upon her, and the quicker the hood is on her head the better.

Possibly, if she is a wild-natured hawk and has been out for a few days, she will not allow any man even within gunshot. The best plan in such a case is to throw out a live pigeon with a long string attached to it which it can carry away pretty well. If the hawk takes this and kills it, go right in upon her, seizing the string, and frighten her off it. She will not go far. The long line must then be set with an ordinary slip-knot round the pigeon, which must be *firmly* pegged down just as the hawk left it; a few wing feathers should be stuck round the noose so as to guide the line upwards and round the hawk's legs. The falconer must retire to the end thereof, conceal himself, and play the game of patience. Sooner or later the hawk is sure to return to her kill, and, if she does so, one pull secures her.

This snare can be set with a long spring of india-rubber and a trigger, so that the lighting of the hawk on the pigeon will liberate it and tighten the noose. If the falconer finds more kills than one, a snare or two of this kind will aid him much.

A very good device for catching a half-hungry hawk that will stoop at a pigeon, half in play, half in earnest, is as follows. A short strap of stout leather is cut, about three inches long by three-quarters of an inch broad ; to this there are attached four or five little snares of catgut, or of gimp, so arranged that, when open, they stand like a series of little wings on a salmon fly, upright, all along the strap, about an inch high. The whole apparatus is next fastened to a pigeon's back by means of double strings round the shoulder of each wing and one round the root of the tail. The strap then fits close along his back among his feathers without impeding his flight in the least, and the snares stand up the whole length of his back and well above it. The pigeon is now thrown out with a long line attached, and should the hawk make but a half-hearted stoop, it is ten to one she will catch her claws in one or other of the snares and be fast. With a pigeon, and a long string attached to her toe, she is readily taken, and we have known even wild hawks to be caught in this way in England. In the East, where they are far tamer, it is almost a certainty.[1]

[1] Should a hawk persistently carry any light quarry, the best plan to adopt is to fly another—a very tame hawk—at her. Both hawks will then hold on to the prey, and the falconer can easily approach. Failing this device, the hawk must either be snared, or else frightened off her quarry, and then taken down in the usual way.

Made in the USA
Columbia, SC
10 December 2017